I Like to Wash My Hands

BY A.J. BOOK

Subjects: | BISAC: JUVENILE NONFICTION / Health & Daily Living / Daily Activities. | JUVENILE NONFICTION / Concepts / Body. | HEALTH & FITNESS / Children's Health.

Library of Congress Control Number: 2020916358
ISBN-13: 978-0-578-74702-6

These are my hands!

Each morning after I use

the bathroom,

I wash my hands.

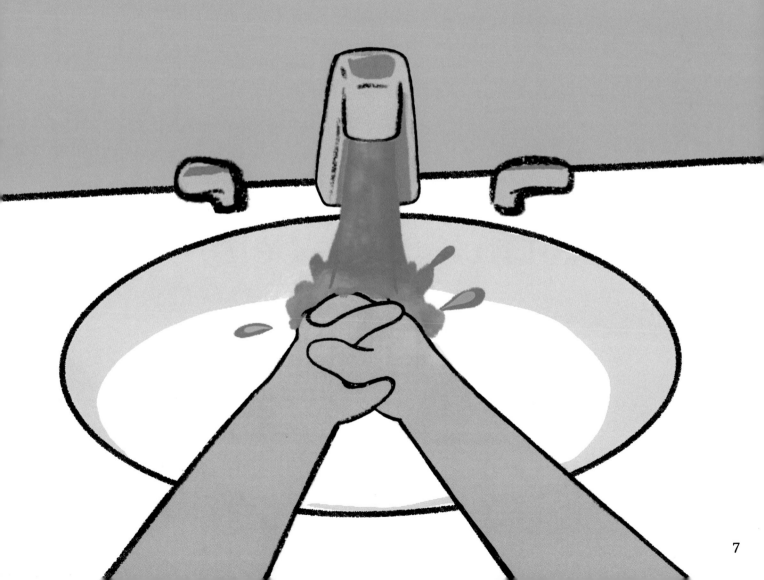

I wash my hands before

lunch at school.

When I come

home,

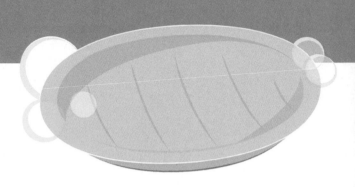

I wash them again.

Sometimes when I turn on the faucet, the water splashes!

I always wash my hands
before dinner.

Every time I use soap.

The soap is so slippery!

Mom says it gets rid of germs that make people sick.

I sing the ABC song while I watch the bubbles!

Then I rinse my hands with

warm water...

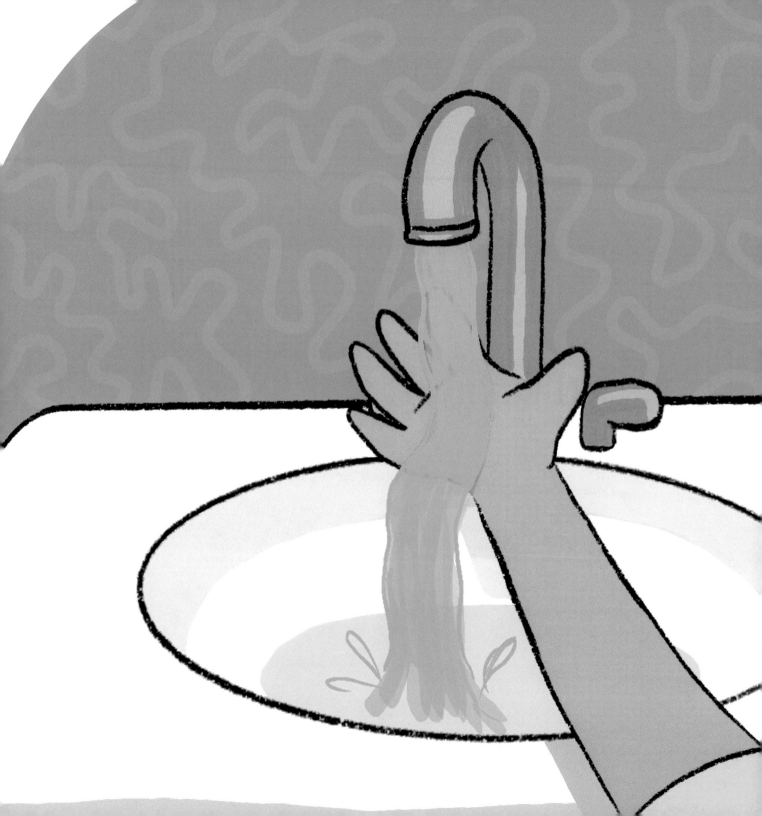

...and turn off the faucet.

I like to dry my hands with
a fuzzy towel.

I hang up the towel,

so it can dry.

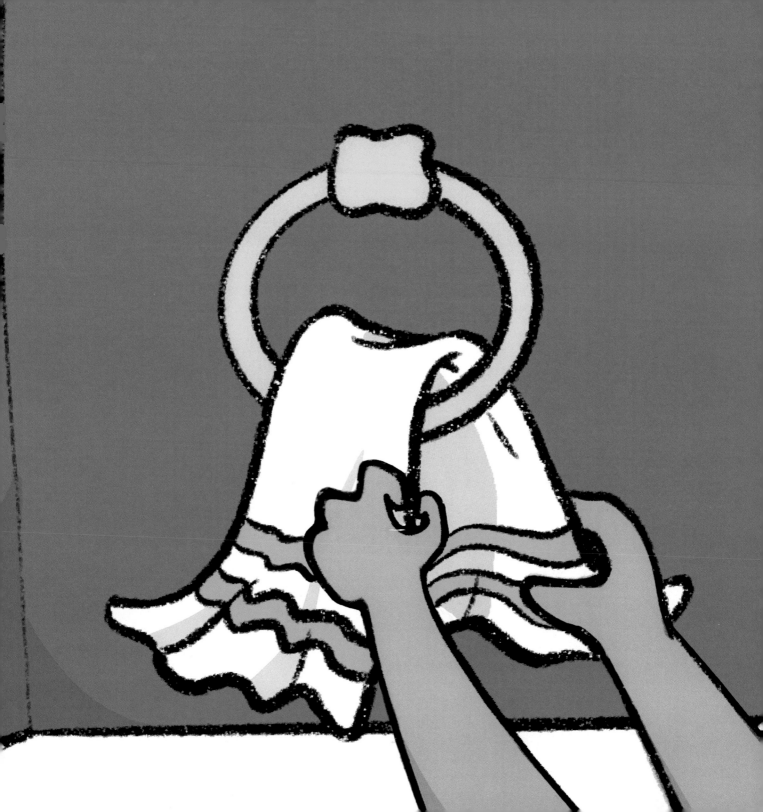

Now my hands are

really clean!

I like to wash my hands.